Art Masterpieces of
THE NATIONAL GALLERY LONDON

Designed and Produced by

TED SMART

and

DAVID GIBBON

COOMBE BOOKS

INTRODUCTION

For millions of Londoners as well as for visitors, both from other parts of Britain and the ever-increasing numbers from the rest of the world, one of the best-known landmarks of the capital is the National Gallery. With its neo-Palladian facade gracing the north side of Trafalgar Square, it looks out towards Nelson's Column and Admiralty Arch and the majestic sweep of Whitehall – a scene that has changed little since the building was formally opened in 1838.

It is probable that few of the visitors who come to view the superb amassment of pictures which is housed here, in the oldest of London's great national collections, realise that there was a great deal of opposition to the establishment of a National Museum of Art when the idea was first mooted towards the end of the 18th century. Even the eminent English landscape painter John Constable, some of whose best-known works are now housed in the gallery, was firmly against the idea and the government of the day also showed little interest. This despite other galleries being already established in Vienna, Paris, Amsterdam, Madrid and Berlin and disregarding the fact that the nucleus of a collection had been offered to the nation by Sir George Beaumont in 1823 – on condition that a suitable building was found in which to house the paintings.

It was not until the following year – 1824 – that the government finally decided to act and this was only because it was discovered that the Prince of Orange was on the point of finalising the purchase of an extensive collection owned by John Julius Angerstein, a Russian-born financier who had recently died.

Influenced by this, and a growing national feeling that the leading world power of the time should have a national gallery to rank with the rest of Europe, the House of Commons voted to allocate the sum of £60,000 for the purchase of the Angerstein collection, together with the lease of his house at number 100, Pall Mall. The Angerstein pictures were joined there by those included in Sir George Beaumont's previous offer together with a similar bequest from the Reverend Holwell Carr.

By 1831 the need for a permanent purpose-built gallery in which to house the rapidly growing collection was evident. In that year William Wilkins' design was accepted and work began in 1833 on the site in Trafalgar Square. This was not before time, as Angerstein's house was in imminent danger of collapse and the collection had to be moved to an even more cramped location at number 105, Pall Mall.

As soon as the new gallery was opened, in 1838, problems became evident. The design of the building was such that there was insufficient space for all the paintings. Extra room was provided in 1876 by the building of a new wing designed by Sir James Barry and this, together with further building work carried out in 1887 and the addition of another wing to balance Barry's, completed in 1911, helped to alleviate the problems. These problems had been further aggravated by the purchase of 76 pictures from the Peel collection, and the Wynn Ellis bequest of 1876 which, whilst providing the gallery with a good representation of Dutch pictures, created further storage problems.

Whereas most of the world's other galleries were originally founded on a royal collection the National Gallery is unique in that its pictures have been collected over the years by purchases on the open market or by bequests from private individuals. Lack of space was not the only problem with which the Keeper and his six-man committee were confronted during the early years. Not only was the choice of acquisitions – which was very much according to personal taste – criticised, but the policy of cleaning pictures also caused an outcry among a population used to seeing Old Masters covered in dirt and layers of discoloured varnish. In order to resolve these problems an enquiry was held in 1853 and the constitution of the gallery was revised. An annual purchase grant was allocated in 1855 and Sir Charles Lock Eastlake was appointed the first Director, with sole responsibility for choosing and acquiring new paintings.

It was subsequently decided that the gallery should be as comprehensive in its coverage of the great periods of art as possible, and whilst many other galleries throughout the world may hold a better selection relating to particular periods, none can match the National Gallery's collection of 2,050 works, predominantly Old Masters, covering all periods.

As a result of the decision to make the National Gallery's collection as comprehensive as possible, nearly all the British paintings were moved to the Tate Gallery at Millbank, which was opened in 1897 to house these and modern foreign works.

During the 19th century it had been possible for the Gallery to acquire many fine paintings at relatively low cost but circumstances began to change and the increasing competition from other galleries, in America and Germany particularly, has made it much more difficult to purchase fine paintings, which now fetch record prices on the world's art market.

In 1975 the opening of the northern extension enabled the gallery's administration to hang the collection in more spacious and restful surroundings, thus adding to the visitor's enjoyment.

In addition to housing the paintings, the gallery also carries out its own restoration work, both of pictures and frames, and with its special exhibitions and projects designed expressly for children it has done much to make art more acceptable and understandable to the general public.

Left is shown a detail from 'The Mystic Nativity'
by Sandro **Botticelli** (c. 1445–1510).

Duccio di Buoninsegna (about 1255–about 1318), the first great painter of the Sienese school, is particularly noted for his purity of line and colour.

'The Annunciation' *above* is one of three predella panels in the gallery forming part of the 'Maestà', Duccio's masterpiece, effected for the High Altar of Siena's Cathedral between 1308 and 1311.

Most of the early works by Italian painters, particularly those of the Sienese school, were commissioned by churches and in consequence are essentially religious in subject.

'The Virgin and Child with Saints' *left* is a further exquisite example of Duccio's refinement of style and is part of a triptych probably painted before 1308.

Pisanello (Antonio di Puccio Pisano) (about 1395-1455) was greatly admired during his lifetime for his meticulous attention to detail and superb drawing, which provides some magnificent examples of painting during the Italian Renaissance.

'The Vision of St Eustace', a detail of which can be seen *right*, contains elements from the International Gothic style and although familiarly thought to be the figure of St Eustace, it has been argued that it was possibly that of St Hubert. This results from the fact that both saints were said to have been converted to Christianity under similar circumstances, in that each had a vision of the Crucifixion whilst out hunting.

The predella panel from an altarpiece *below* is the work of the early Italian painter **Giovanni** di Paolo (c 1403–1482).

The wing of a tryptych *left*, called 'St John The Baptist and St Jerome', is ascribed to **Masolino** da Panicale (c 1383–after 1432), whose work was closely associated with that of Masaccio.

Fra **Angelico** (Guido di Pietro) (before 1400?-1455) was a deeply religious man whose compassion and gentleness is clearly recognisable in his art. 'Christ Glorified in the Court of Heaven' *below* is the centre panel of the predella from an altarpiece painted c 1435.

'The Annunciation' *above right* is the work of Fra Filippo **Lippi** (about 1406-1469). A member of the Carmelite Order of Monks, until he was released from his vows to marry a nun, he was much patronised by the powerful Medici family.

Paolo **Uccello** (P. di Dono) (c 1397-1475) worked mainly in Florence and entered the Physicians Guild of Florence in 1415. A painter who was greatly interested in perspective, his own particular style is evident in 'Niccolò Mauruzi da Tolentino at the Battle of San Romano' *right*.

'The Virgin and Child with the Magdalen and St John the Baptist' *above* is an altarpiece painted on canvas by Andrea **Mantegna** (c 1430/31-1506). For many years this brilliant artist was Court Painter to the Gonzaga family at Mantua.

Ascribed to the brothers Antonio and Piero del **Pollaiuolo** (c 1432-1498 & c 1441-1496) the altarpiece 'The Martyrdom of St Sebastian' *right* was commissioned by the Pucci family for the Oratory of S. Sebastiano attached to the church of the SS. Annunziata in Florence.

'A Concert' *top left* is an early work on wood by Lorenzo **Costa** (c1459/60–1535) of the Ferrarese school.

Piero della Francesca (after 1420–1492) was a Tuscan whose early work *above left* 'The Baptism of Christ' is believed to be a part of an altarpiece. During the later years of his life Piero spent his time studying perspective and mathematics, possibly because his failing eyesight made it difficult for him to continue painting.

The heavily decorated work of Carlo Giovanni **Crivelli** (c1435/40–1493) *far left*, 'The Annunciation with St Emidius', was painted in commemoration of a papal grant, bestowed on the people of Ascoli Piceno, in 1482.

Antonello da Messina (about 1430–1479) was one of the first Italians to use oil paint and in consequence greatly influenced Venetian painting. His 'Portrait of a Man', believed to be a self-portrait, is shown *left*.

'The Agony in the Garden' *above* and 'The Doge Leonardo Loredan' *right* are both brilliant executions by Giovanni **Bellini** (about 1430–1516), the son of Jacopo Bellini.

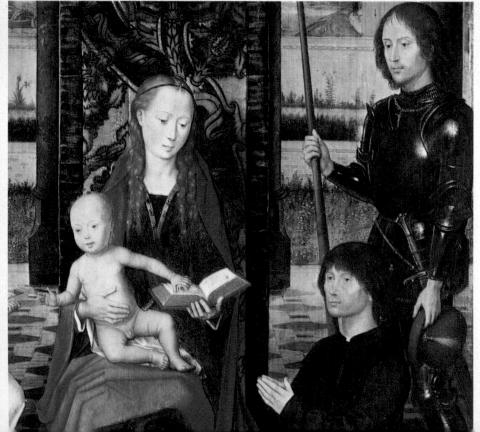

'The Wilton Diptych' (c 1395 or later) *above and above left* is attributed to the French school, although its International Gothic style precludes any final hypothesis on the subject. The diptych depicts 'Richard II Presented to the Virgin and Child by His Patron Saints' but little is known about the circumstances or date of its execution, or the artist's nationality.

Although the 'Virgin and Child with an Angel, St George and Donor' *left* is similar to the centre panel of Hans **Memlinc**'s (active 1465 died 1494) 'The Donne Triptych', the quality of the work is inferior and would therefore appear to be the work of his Studio, rather than of the painter himself.

'A Woman' *right* is one of a pair of companion portraits of a man and a woman, ascribed to Robert **Campin** (c 1378/79–1444), who worked in Tournai from 1406 and is presumed to have been of Flemish origin.

'The Arnolfini Marriage' *below*, by Jan van **Eyck** (active 1422 died 1441), is indicative of the artist's love of rich colour and detailed intricacy. The founder of the Bruges school, he was also Court Painter to Philip the Good, Duke of Burgundy.

The portrait of 'A Little Girl' *right* is thought to be Jacqueline, the daughter of a patron of the artist Jan **Gossaert,** called **Mabuse** (c 1478–1532).

'The Adoration of the Kings' *above* is a further painting, on oak, by Jan **Gossaert**, and is believed to have been painted after c 1500.

Hieronymus **Bosch** (about 1450–1516), an outstanding innovator amongst Flemish artists, is probably most widely known for his paintings depicting macabre and illusory situations, and whilst the majority of his work is of a religious nature, see *top right* 'Christ Mocked', the full scope of his originality is clearly discernible in all his art.

The painting on canvas by Bartholomaeus **Spranger** (1546–1611) *above right*, entitled 'The Adoration of the Kings' was executed whilst he was in the service of the Hapsburg Emperors, c 1595.

Pictured *right* is an unconventional representation of 'The Adoration of the Kings', by Jan **Brueghel I** (1568–1625), the son of Pieter Brueghel the Elder.

Lucas **Cranach** the Elder (1472–1553), considered to be the most talented painter of the German Reformation, was also a close friend of Martin Luther, whom he met in Wittenburg. His use of pale colours highlighting the delicate, stylised forms is beautifully illustrated in 'Cupid Complaining to Venus' *above left*.

The portrait *above* is believed to be that of 'St Ivo', and possibly a panel from a diptych or similar structure. It was painted by Rogier van der **Weyden** (1399–1464), who was a notable pupil of Robert Campin at Tournai, between 1426–32.

'The Ambassadors' *left* was painted by Hans **Holbein** the Younger (1497/8–1543) and depicts the French Ambassador, Jean de Dinteville and his friend, Georges de Selve, Bishop of Lavour.

Of all the great artists of the German school, Albrecht **Dürer** (1471–1528) was undoubtedly supreme. This man of genius was also a printmaker, goldsmith, and author of various artistic treatises. 'The Painter's Father' *right* is ascribed to his name.

Raphael (Raffaello Santı) (c
1483–1520) died in Rome aged 37
and the tragic, early death of this
sensitive artist was a loss of
magnitude to the world of art. A
contempory of da Vinci and
Michelangelo, by whom he was
greatly influenced, he had, by the
age of 28, already established
himself as a serious rival to both
of these great men. Two of his
celebrated works can be seen
above, 'St Catherine of Alexandria'
and *above left*, 'Pope Julius II'.

The delicate, moving work of
'The Virgin and Child with St
Anne and St John the Baptist' *right*
is indicative of the aesthetic and
artistic brilliance of the executor,
Leonardo da Vinci (c 1452–1519).
This accomplished man was a
painter, architect, sculptor and
military engineer, whose legacy to
the world includes thousands of
drawings and notebooks, which
record both his scientific and
artistic experiments. 'The Virgin
(or Madonna) of the Rocks' *left* is
one of two versions, one of which
is contained in the Gallery and the
other in the Louvre in Paris.

The embodiment of spiritual love is shown in the early work by Antonio Allegri da **Correggio** (c 1489/94–1534) *above left* in his 'Mercury Instructing Cupid before Venus' ("The School of Love").

One of the most celebrated Portraitists of his day, the Florentine painter, Agnolo **Bronzino** (c 1503–1572) was also an exponent of Mannerist art. His panel painting, 'An Allegory', is shown *above*.

Michelangelo Buonarrotti (c 1475–1564) painter, sculptor, and architect, was a brilliant man who became a legend in his own lifetime. His respect for antiquity is readily discernible in his supreme achievements and, although 'The Entombment', an unfinished work *left*, is believed to be that of the great artist, its attribution has been questioned.

'The Raising of Lazarus' *right* was executed by Sebastiano Luciani called **Sebastiano** del Piombo (c 1485–1547), of the Venetian school.

Parmigianino, a Parmesan painter of great importance, also painted 'The Mystic Marriage of St Catherine' *above*.

Titian (Tiziano Vecellio) (about c 1487/90–1576) was born Pieve di Cadore and with his tremendous artistic capacity which he developed over the years, the Venetian Renaissance achieved its pinnacle of perfection. Two of his great masterpieces can be seen in the 'Portrait of a Man' *below* and 'Bacchus and Ariadne' *above right*.

'The Story of Aristaeus' *below right* is ascribed to **Niccolo** dell 'Abate (c 1509/12–1571), who was originally from Modena.

'Madonna and Child with St John the Baptist and St Jerome' *above* is an altarpiece by **Parmigianino** (Girolamo Francesco Maria Mazzola) (c 1503–1540).

The 'Holy Family with the Infant Baptist' *left* was painted by one of the most important artists of the period, Federico **Baroccio** (c about 1535–1612), from Urbino.

Veronese (Paolo Caliari) (1528–1588), a contemporary of Tintoretto, was one of the most prolific decorators of his period, when established in Venice. The artist's preoccupation with colour and texture resulted in a sumptuousness beloved by Venetian taste, which is evident in his superb rendering of 'The Family of Darius before Alexander' *above*.

One of the leading Venetian artists of his day, Jacopo **Tintoretto** (1518–1594) executed 'The Origin of the Milky Way' *right*, most probably during the late 1570's. The milk which was spilled from the breasts of Juno when Hercules' mother, Alcmene, attempted to immortalise the infant, is said to have been the origin of the 'Milky Way'.

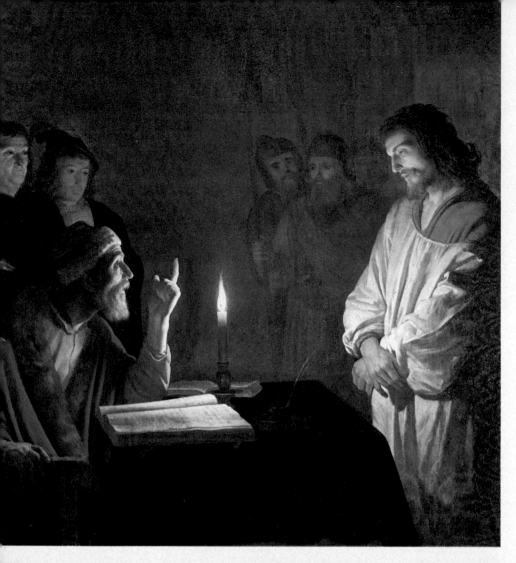

Born in Utrecht, where he studied
under Bloemaert, Gerrit van
Honthorst (c 1590–1656) was a
highly regarded portrait painter of
his time, and his 'Christ before the
High Priest' *left*, became one of the
most renowned paintings in
Rome.

The early work of Hendrick
Avercamp (c 1685–1634), 'A
Winter scene with skaters near a
Castle' *right*, is typical of the winter
landscapes for which he is
famous.

Frans **Hals** (c 1581/5–1666), an
outstanding portrait painter of the
new Dutch Republic, introduced
an entirely new style, which was to
pave the way for a franker and
more natural approach to portrait
painting. 'Family Group in a
Landscape' *below* is a superb
example of his work.

Rembrandt (Harmensz van Rijn) (1606–1669), the son of a rich Leyden miller, studied under Pieter Lastman in Amsterdam and became one of the most outstanding and accomplished artists ever to rival any of the great masters. His sense of drama and superb mastery of chiaroscuro combine to produce a passionate realism which radiates from all his paintings.

The portrait *above* 'Hendrickje Stoffels' and the 'Self-Portrait aged Sixty-three' *left*, are indicative of his magnificent brushwork and depth of colour.

'Belshazzar's Feast' *above* and 'A Woman Bathing in a Stream' *left* are two further outstanding examples showing the rich quality of **Rembrandt**'s work.

Jan van **Cappelle** (c 1623/25–1679) belonged to a group of Netherland landscape artists, originating in the 17th century, in Haarlem, who specialised in seascapes and more specifically in marine subjects. The soft, sombre hues, beautifully illustrated in his 'A Shipping Scene with a Dutch Yacht firing a Salute' *above right*, are in direct contrast to the highly coloured works of the earlier Dutch masters.

Typical of Italianistic landscapes of the period, diffusing quiet, gentle tones across the canvas, is 'A Rocky Landscape with an Ox-cart' *right*, painted by Jan **Both** (c 1618?–1652).

The careful precision of the work of Johannes **Vermeer** (c 1632–1675), which can be seen above in 'Young Woman standing at a Virginal', has been compared to a photographic reproduction, and the implication follows that he might possibly have used some mechanical aid, such as a camera obscura, for achieving his end results.

One of the most skilful landscape artists of his generation, Aelbert **Cuyp** (c 1620–1691) was greatly influenced by the use of light imbued in the paintings of both Rembrandt and Claude. 'A Hilly River Landscape' *above right* includes the artist's penchant for a herd of cattle set before a distant scene, preferably that of his home town, Dordrecht.

Meyndert **Hobbema** (c 1638–1709) was a pupil of Jacob van Ruisdael, and although a superb draughtsman, his specialist activities were confined within somewhat narrow lines. However, his most famous landscape, 'The Avenue, Middelharnis' *right* is a magnificent example of his ability to capture, on canvas, with precision, all the freshness that his clarity of vision beheld.

Peeter Pauwel **Rubens** (c 1577–1640) was a genius whose talents combined to make him one of the most justly revered of all painters. This incredible man was also a devout Catholic and he produced a prolific number of works for churches and palaces throughout Europe. Whilst his traditionalist sympathies are evident in his compositions, the dynamism and drama are also clearly visible and this in turn evokes a feeling of enthusiasm so obviously felt by this great artist.

Three examples can be seen here showing the accomplished diversity of his talents: 'The Judgement of Paris' *above left*, 'Autumn Landscape with a View of Het Steen' *left* and 'Susanna Lunden, "Le Chapeau de Paille"' *above*.

Anthony van **Dyck** (c 1599–1641), although influenced early in his career by Rubens, later developed a quieter and more refined style which in turn was to have a profound effect on portrait painting in England, lasting until the end of the 18th century. He was court painter to Charles I, by whom he was knighted in 1632, and the 'Equestrian Portrait of Charles I' *right*, is one of his most celebrated works. Another exquisite example can be seen *left* in 'A Woman and Child', showing the rich attire of the Cavalier court.

The portrait *above left* is of 'Govaert van Surpele and his Wife', executed by Jacob **Jordaens** (c 1593–1678), who became, after the demise of Rubens and van Dyck, the most celebrated figure painter of the southern Netherlands.

'A Boy Aged Eleven' *above* is a lovely example of the work of portrait and figure painter Jacob van **Oost** I (1601–1671).

The most eminent of all Spanish artists, Diego Rodriguez de Silva y **Velázquez** (c 1599–1660) was born and trained in Seville and over the years his developments and achievements were phenomenal. The only surviving painting of a female nude by Velázquez is 'The Toilet of Venus, "The Rokeby Venus"' *above,* and *right* is shown a detail from 'Kitchen Scene with Christ in the House of Martha and Mary'.

One of the most influential Italian artists of the 17th century, Michelangelo Merisi de **Caravaggio** (c 1573–1610), was a controversial figure who was constantly invoking the wrath of law and authority. His dramatic work, however, bears the stamp of originality and this is superbly reflected in 'The Supper at Emmaus' shown *above left.*

Nicolas **Poussin** (c 1594–1665) was a man of high intellect whose range encompassed a rich variety of subjects. 'A Bacchanalian Revel' *left* is believed to have been painted during the latter part of the 1630's.

One of the few signed works by **Velázquez**, 'Philip IV of Spain in Brown and Silver' is shown *above left*.

The representation of 'St Margaret' as a shepherdess *above* was executed by the Spanish artist, Francisco de **Zurbaran** (c 1598–1664).

Although **El Greco** (Domenikos Theotokopoulos) (c 1541–1614) was born in Crete, his was the genius which founded Spain as an artistic centre. One of his magnificent paintings can be seen *left* 'Christ driving the Traders from the Temple'.

Most of the work of Bartolome Esteban **Murillo** (c 1617–1682) is mainly religious in essence and 'The Two Trinities' ("The Pedroso Murillo") *right* is from the collection of the Marques del Pedroso.

Giovanni Battista **Pittoni** (c 1687–1767) was one of the foremost historical artists of his era and 'The Nativity with God the Father and the Holy Ghost' *above left* is an excellent example of his work.

A leading decorative painter of the period, whose painting of 'Bacchus and Ariadne' is shown *above*, was Sebastiano **Ricci** (c 1659–1734), born at Belluno.

'A Caprice with Ruins on the Seashore' *left*, executed by Francesco **Guardi** (c 1712–1793), is a beautiful example of the artist's delicate use of colour and whose success lay largely in his magical paintings of Venice.

One of the most commercially successful painters of his time, **Canaletto** (Giovanni Antonio Canale) (1697–1768), was particularly popular with English visitors to Venice. Two of his fine Venetian views can be seen, *above right* 'Campo St Vidal and St Maria della Carita' (The Stonemason's Yard') and *right* 'The Basin of St Marco on Ascension Day'.

'Manon Balletti' *left* is the work of Jean-Marc **Nattier** (c 1685–1766), a fashionable portrait painter at the court of Louis XV.

The delicate, ethereal settings beloved by Jean-Antoine **Watteau** (c 1684–1721), an example of which can be seen *right* in a detail from 'La Gamme d'Amour', are poignant reminders of the untimely death of this romantic artist, at the age of thirty-seven.

Inspired by Watteau and subsequently one of the more notable of the 'fêtes galantes' painters, was Nicolas **Lancret** (c 1690–1743), whose charming painting of 'A Lady and Gentleman with Two Girls in a Garden' ("La Tasse de Chocolat") is shown *below*.

The exquisite 'Landscape with a Watermill' *above left* is the brushwork of François **Boucher** (1703–1770), an indefatigable and gifted artist, who became 'First Painter to the King' under Louis XV.

Claude-Joseph **Vernet** (c 1714–1789), a member of the Académie at Paris, was also the foremost landscape and marine painter of the period. 'A Seashore' *left* was painted in 1776 for the Comte de Luc.

The distinguished artist George **Stubbs** (c 1724–1806) is best known for his superb paintings of horses. 'The Milbanke and Melbourne Families' *above* shows his acute powers of observation and meticulous attention to detail.

William **Hogarth** (1697–1764) is often referred to as the 'Father of English Painting' and as a product of the 'Age of Reason' his work frequently reflects his moral attitudes to society in the new era of enlightenment. The delightful portrait *right* is entitled 'The Shrimp Girl'.

Thomas **Gainsborough** (c 1727–1788) is a name synonymous with 18th century portraiture and together with his contemporary and rival, Sir Joshua Reynolds, he produced for English society a plethora of 'likenesses' for which both were handsomely rewarded. 'The Morning Walk' *right* and 'Mr and Mrs Andrews' *above* show the artist's delight in portraying the naturalness of his subjects, which also embraces an elegance of attire, set against tranquil, Georgian backgrounds. Gainsborough's love for the sensuality of music, rather than an intellectual leaning towards literature, is often strongly reflected in the many magnificent examples of his work.

Landscape painting, however, was his first love and his charming, idyllic scenes, such as the exquisite 'The Watering Place' *left*, show perfect rural settings and the harmony between man and nature.

Sir Joshua **Reynolds** (c 1723–
1792) has already been mentioned
as an outstanding 18th century
painter, and he was appointed
President of the Royal Academy
on its foundation in 1768. The
painting *above left* of 'General Sir
Banastre Tarleton' is a fine
portrait by this eminent artist.

The infant prodigy Sir Thomas
Lawrence (c 1769–1830) painted
the full-length portrait of 'Queen
Charlotte' shown *above*.

'The Duke of Wellington' *right* is
the work of the incomparable
Francisco de **Goya** (y Lucientes)
(c 1746–1828). This man of
genius, whose ability to portray
the human condition beyond the
limitations of time and situation
and whose work still continues to
inspire, was tragically struck deaf
by a severe illness in 1792.

A further outstanding painting by
Hogarth is 'The Countess's
Morning Levée' *left*, one of a
series entitled 'Marriage à la
Mode'.

'The Haywain' *left,* one of the most famous of all the paintings by John **Constable** (1776–1837), was exhibited at the Paris Salon in 1824 where it was met by rapturous applause, and Constable was awarded a gold medal by Charles X. 'Salisbury Cathedral and Archdeacon Fisher's House' *above left,* a further work by this great and gifted artist shows the brilliant use of his broken brushwork, which, through Delacroix, was to greatly influence European art.

Joseph Mallord William **Turner** (c 1775–1851), a magnificent 19th century painter of nature, was fascinated by the emotional effect of light, which features significantly in all his paintings. His canvasses glow with colour and are seen to perfection in both 'Rain, Steam, and Speed – The Great Western Railway' *right,* and 'The Fighting Téméraire' *above,* one of his most spectacular works.

The artistic movement originating in Paris, in the 1860's, and known as 'Impressionism' was based on the artistic premise that it was possible to capture, on canvas, the natural and spontaneous feeling or 'impression' evoked by the landscape.

Claude-Oscar **Monet** (c 1840–1926), considered to be the most gifted in the field of landscape painting, used lighter and bolder colours to convey the emotional freshness of the scene. 'The Water-Lily Pond' *above* is one of a series of the artist's garden at Giverny, whilst *left* is shown a detail from 'The Beach at Trouville'.

Édouard **Manet** (c 1832–1883), who was particularly influenced by Goya, was the most conservative member of the movement. 'The Waitress', a detail of which can be seen *right*, is on two pieces of vertically joined canvas.

'The Côtes des Boeufs at L'Hermitage near Pontoise' *above* is the work of Camille **Pissarro** (c1830–1903) who, as one of the major figures at the formation of the Impressionist group, was a determining factor in the development of the movement.

Another leading member of the movement from its inception was Pierre-August **Renoir** (c1841–1919), whose greatest achievement lay in his portrayal of the female nude. Like Monet his landscapes are invocative of riverbank scenes along the Seine. 'The Umbrellas' *right* was believed to have been completed after Renoir had paid a visit to Italy between 1881 and 1882.

One of the greatest painters of the Post-Impressionist period, Henri **Toulouse-Lautrec** (c 1864–1901) was sadly crippled from childhood. His vivid paintings of the dancers and singers who performed in the music halls and bars in Paris which he frequented, rank among the best of his work. 'Woman seated in a Garden' *left* was painted in the garden of Monsieur Forest.

'Combing the Hair' *below* is an unfinished work by Hilaire-Germain Edgar **Degas** (c 1834–1917), an Impressionist who is probably most famous for his paintings of ballet dancers.

Paul **Gauguin** (c 1848–1903) also ranks amongst the best of the Post-Impressionists, and he constantly strove to achieve a rich combination of form and colour. 'Flower-piece' *right* was painted in Tahiti during 1896.

Henri Rousseau

Although Paul **Cézanne** (c 1839–1906) is generally grouped with the Impressionists, he was, in essence, a Post-Impressionist painter in that he sought to emphasise content and structure, whilst at the same time retaining all the original benefits gained by the early Impressionist movement. 'An Old Woman with a Rosary' *right* is a mature work by this much imitated artist, and *left* can be seen 'Mountains in Provence', also painted during his later years.

'Tropical Storm with a Tiger' *above*, the work of Henri **Rousseau** ('le Douanier') (c 1844–1910) was the first in a series of jungle scenes by the artist, who is considered to be the foremost painter in the group known as the 'modern primitives'.

The full-length portrait of 'Hermine Gallica' *overleaf* was painted by the Austrian artist Gustav **Klimt** (c 1862–1918) during 1904.

First published in Great Britain 1978 by Colour Library International Ltd.
© Illustrations reproduced by courtesy of the Trustees, The National Gallery, London.
Colour separations by La Cromolito, Milan, Italy.
Display and text filmsetting by Focus Photoset, London, England.
Printed in Spain by CAYFOSA
bound by EUROBINDER-Barcelona
ISBN 0 904681 87 4